DELANEY
STREET
PRESS

Mothers Change
the World...
One Child
at a Time

Mothers Change the World...
One Child at a Time

By Mary Carlisle Beasley

DELANEY STREET PRESS
Nashville, TN: (800) 256-8584

ISBN 1-58334-058-0

The ideas expressed in this book are not, in all cases, exact quotations, as some have been edited for clarity and brevity. In all cases, the author has attempted to maintain the speaker's original intent. In some cases, material for this book was obtained from secondary sources, primarily print media. While every effort was made to ensure the accuracy of these sources, the accuracy cannot be guaranteed. For additions, deletions, corrections or clarifications in future editions of this text, please write DELANEY STREET PRESS.

Printed in the United States of America
1 2 3 4 5 6 7 8 9 10 • 00 01 02 03 04

Cover by Bart Dawson
Typesetting by Sue Gerdes

ACKNOWLEDGMENTS

The author gratefully acknowledges the helpful support of Angela Beasley Freeman, Dick and Mary Freeman, Mary Susan Freeman, Carli Freeman, Jim Gallery, and the entire team of professionals at DELANEY STREET PRESS and WALNUT GROVE PRESS.

For Angela Beasley Freeman

Table of Contents

Mothers Change the World...
One Child at a Time

Motherhood, without question, is the world's most important occupation: Mothers shape the whole of mankind as they shape the lives of their children. Abraham Lincoln spoke for grateful children everywhere when he observed, "All that I am, or all that I hope to be, I owe to my angel mother."

This little book celebrates the importance of motherhood and the timeless value of the lessons that mothers teach. On the pages that follow, we consider eight of the most important lessons that mothers have shared since the dawn of humanity. Principles such as these are a priceless bequest.

It has been said that the hand that rocks the cradle rules the world. Such is the unending power of motherhood. Thus, we all owe the greatest possible debt to those women who continue to change the world one child at a time.

Of all the rights of women, the greatest
is to be a mother.
Lin Yutang

The woman who creates and sustains
a home is a creator second to none.
Helen Hunt Jackson

Mothers are the most important actors
in the grand drama of human progress.
Elizabeth Cady Stanton

A mother is...
the holiest thing alive.

Samuel Taylor Coleridge

The mother is the
uncharted servant
of the future.

Katherine Anthony

Every mother is like Moses. She does not enter the promised land. She prepares a world she will not see.

Pope Paul VI

Her children arise up and call her blessed.

Proverbs 31:28

Mother is the name for God on the lips and in the hearts of little children.

William Makepeace Thackery

God could not be everywhere, so He made mothers.

Jewish Proverb

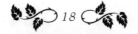

18

Mother's Lesson #1:

Love

The first lesson a caring mother teaches her child is the lesson of love. A mother's love is like no other, a gift that is freely given, demonstrated by deed and by word.

In this chapter, we consider a collection of thoughtful quotations that would make any mother proud. The following words of wisdom remind us of the everlasting importance of a little four-letter word that changes everything. That word — as mothers know perfectly well — is love.

Love yourself first and everything else
falls into line. You really have to love
yourself to get anything done
in this world.

Lucille Ball

The story of a love is not important —
what is important is that one is capable
of love. It is perhaps the only glimpse
we are permitted of eternity.

Helen Hayes

Love is a multiplication.

Marjory Stoneman Douglas

Whoever loves true life
will love true love.
Elizabeth Barrett Browning

Nobody has ever measured, not even
poets, how much the heart can hold.
Zelda Fitzgerald

Love is a game that two can play
and both win.
Eva Gabor

The best and most
beautiful things in the
world cannot be seen
or even touched.
They must be felt
with the heart.

Helen Keller

Accustom yourself continually to make many acts of love, for they enkindle and melt the soul.

Saint Teresa of Avila

Love is not a state, it is a direction.

Simone Weil

Love is a great beautifier.

Louisa May Alcott

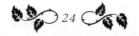

A woman who is loved
always has success.

Vicki Baum

Love doesn't just sit there like a stone; it has to be made, like bread, remade all the time, made new.

Ursula K. Le Guin

All love that has not friendship
for its base is like a mansion built
upon the sand.
Ella Wheeler Wilcox

Love will not always linger longest
with those who hold it in
too clenched a fist.
Alice Duer Miller

The best proof of love is trust.
Dr. Joyce Brothers

There is only one terminal dignity — love.

Helen Hayes

Until I truly loved, I was alone.

Caroline Norton

The giving of love is an education
in itself.

Anonymous

Love conquers all except poverty
and toothaches.

Mae West

To love is to receive a glimpse of heaven.
Karen Sunde

Mother's Lesson #2:

Family

Who more than a mother understands the importance of family? After all, a family is a mother's creation (accomplished, of course, with the obvious participation of father).

Mothers change the world one family at a time. Family life is the foundation of human existence, and mother is the cornerstone. As Anna Trevisan correctly observed, "The mother! She is what keeps the family intact. It is proved. A fact." On the pages that follow, we consider timeless advice for keeping the family happy, healthy, and, above all, together.

The family – that dear octopus from
whose tentacles we never quite escape,
nor, in our innermost hearts,
ever quite wish to.

Dodie Smith

Call it a clan, call it a network, call it
a tribe, call it a family. Whatever you
call it, whoever you are, you need one.

Jane Howard

A family is one of
nature's masterpieces.

George Santayana

Family is the we of me.

Carson McCullers

A family is the first and essential cell
of human society.

Pope John XXIII

No kingdom divided can stand —
neither can a household.

Christine de Pisan

Family life! The United Nations is
child's play compared to the tugs and
splits and need to understand and forgive
in any family.

May Sarton

America's future will be determined by the home and the school. The child becomes largely what he is taught; hence, we must watch what we teach and how we live.

Jane Addams

Family life is the source of the greatest human happiness.

Robert J. Gavinghurst

It takes a heap of livin' in a house to make it home.

Edgar A. Guest

 35

A family is a school of duties...
founded on love.

Felix Adler

Children are the hands by which
we take hold of heaven.

Henry Ward Beecher

The mother's heart is the child's
schoolroom.

Henry Ward Beecher

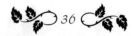

A happy family is but an earlier heaven.

Sir John Bowring

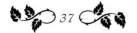

A large family gives beauty to a house.
Indian Proverb

A family divided against itself
will perish together.
Indian Proverb

When the whole family is together,
the soul is at peace.
Russian Proverb

Cherish your human connections —
your relationships with friends and family.
Barbara Bush

You leave home to seek your fortune,
and when you get it, you go home and
share it with your family.
Anita Baker

Family jokes, though rightly cursed
by strangers, are the bond that keeps
most families alive.
Stella Benson

 39

Healthy families are our greatest national resource.

Dolores Curran

The family is the nucleus of civilization.
Will and Ariel Durant

Our children are not going to be just "our children" they are going to be other people's husbands and wives and the parents of our grandchildren.
Mary Steichen Calderone

You don't choose your family. They are God's gift to you, as you are to them.
Desmond Tutu

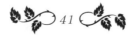

What families have in common the world around is that they are the place where people learn who they are and how to be that way.

Jean Illsley Clarke

The debt of gratitude we owe our mother and father goes forward, not backward. What we owe our parents is the bill presented to us by our children.

Nancy Friday

The best things you can give children,
next to good habits, are good memories.
Sydney J. Harris

Home, in one form or another,
is the great objective of life.
Josiah Gilbert Holland

The happiest moments of my life have
been spent in the bosom of my family.
Thomas Jefferson

When a marriage works, nothing
on earth can take its place.
Helen Gahagan Douglas

All men are different.
All husbands are the same.
Old-Time Saying

Most men need more love
than they deserve.
Marie von Ebner-Eschenbach

Marriage is a covered dish.
Swiss Proverb

A successful marriage requires
falling in love many times, always with
the same person.
Mignon McLaughlin

A successful marriage is not a gift;
it is an achievement.
Ann Landers

A child is a beam of sunlight from the Infinite and Eternal.

Lyman Abbott

A family is a unit composed not only of children, but of men, women, an occasional animal, and the common cold.

Ogden Nash

Children have more need of models than critics.

Joseph Joubert

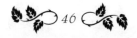

A child is the greatest poem ever known.
Christopher Morley

A baby is God's opinion that the world should go on.
Carl Sandburg

It is not enough for parents to understand children. They must accord children the privilege of understanding them.
Milton R. Sapirstein

Keep your family from the abominable practice of backbiting.

The Old Farmer's Almanac, 1811

Mother's Lesson #3:

Kindness

Henry Ward Beecher noted, "What the mother sings to the cradle goes all the way down to the coffin." Beecher understood that a mother's voice carries a powerful message to her young child. Wise mothers voice their words in a spirit of kindness, thus teaching by example a lesson that lasts a lifetime.

Women from every generation understand the power of a kind word and the value of a helping hand. The following words of wisdom remind us that mother is right: Kindness is the best policy, now and always.

If you stop to be kind,
you must swerve often
from your path.

Mary Webb

Scatter seeds
of kindness.

George Ade

No act of kindness, no matter
how small, is ever wasted.

Aesop

The purpose of human life is to serve
and to show compassion and
the will to help others.

Albert Schweitzer

Life is an exciting business and
most exciting when lived
for other people.

Helen Keller

Kind words can be short and easy to speak, but their echoes are truly endless.

Mother Teresa

Always try to be
a little kinder
than necessary.

J. M. Barrie

The love of our neighbor in all its fullness
simply means being able to say,
"What are you going through?"
Simone Weil

Compassion abolishes the distance
between human beings.
Hannah Arendt

Kindness is the language which the deaf
can hear and the blind can see.
Mark Twain

Life is short and we never have enough
time for the hearts of those who travel the
way with us. O, be swift to love!
Make haste to be kind.

Henri Frédéric Amiel

Love is not getting but giving.

Henry Van Dyke

There is no love which does not
become help.

Paul Tillich

Mother's Lesson #4:

Faith

A Spanish proverb states, "An ounce of mother is worth a ton of priest." This saying reminds us of the profound influence of a mother's presence. At no time is a mother more influential than when she teaches her child the wisdom and the power of faith.

Wise mothers understand that faith serves as a spiritual and emotional beacon in times of hardship; thoughtful mothers share that message with their children; wise children take the message to heart.

Faith can put a candle
      in the darkest night.
             Margaret Sangster

Seeds of faith are always within us;
sometimes it takes a crisis to nourish
    and encourage their growth.
             Susan L. Taylor

Faith is what makes life bearable.
             Madeleine L'Engle

Faith is a spiritual spotlight that illuminates one's path.

Helen Keller

Faith is an activity. It is something that has to be applied.

Corrie ten Boom

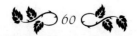

To have courage for whatever comes in life — everything lies in that.

Saint Teresa of Avila

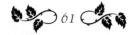

Faith is the only known cure for fear.
Lena Sadler

Keep your face to the sunshine
and you cannot see the shadows.
Helen Keller

God's gifts put
man's best gifts to shame.
Elizabeth Barrett Browning

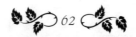

Faith sees the invisible, believes the
unbelievable, and receives the impossible.
Corrie ten Boom

Faith wears everyday clothes and proves
herself in life's ordinary circumstances.
Bertha Munro

Faith is like radar that sees through the
fog — the reality of things at a distance
that the human eye cannot see.
Corrie ten Boom

Faith is the key that
fits the door
of hope.

Elaine Emans

Without faith, nothing is possible.
With it, nothing is impossible.
Mary McLeod Bethune

There are no hopeless situations;
there are only people who have
grown hopeless.
Clare Boothe Luce

My recipe for life is not being
afraid of myself.
Eartha Kitt

Nothing in life is to be feared.
It is only to be understood.
Marie Curie

Sad soul, take comfort nor forget,
the sunrise never failed us yet.
Celia Thaxter

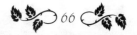

Mother's Lesson #5:

Courage

It takes courage to be a mom. Mothers face the formidable task of giving birth to a child and the even more formidable task of caring for it. Motherhood is no place for sissies.

Amelia Earhart understood the value of heroism when she observed, "Courage is the price that life exacts for granting peace. The soul that knows it not knows no release from little things."

Mother couldn't have said it better herself.

Fear brings out the worst in everybody.
Maya Angelou

Courage is fear that has said its prayers.
Dorothy Bernard

A woman must not accept; she must
challenge. She must not be awed by that
which has been built up around her;
she must revere the woman in her
which struggles for expression.
Margaret Sanger

 68

Do not borrow trouble
by dreading tomorrow.
It is the dark menace of
the future that makes
cowards of us all.

Dorothy Dix

I've always grown from my problems
and from the things that didn't work out.
That's when I've really learned.

Carol Burnett

It takes as much courage to have tried
and failed as it does to have tried
and succeeded.

Anne Morrow Lindbergh

Pain nourishes courage. You can't be
brave if you've only had wonderful
things happen to you.

Mary Tyler Moore

When you get into a really tight place
an everything goes against you, till it
seems as though you could not hang on
a minute longer, never give up then;
for that is just the place and time
that the tide will turn.

Harriet Beecher Stowe

Become so wrapped up in something
that you forget to be afraid.

Lady Bird Johnson

To get it right, be born with luck or else
make it. Never give up. Get the knack of
getting people to help you and
also pitch in yourself.

Ruth Gordon

There is no chance, no destiny, no fate
that can hinder or control the firm
resolve of a determined soul.
Ella Wheeler Wilcox

Challenges make you discover things
about yourself that you never really knew.
They're what make you stretch
and go beyond the norm.
Cicely Tyson

Luck? I don't know anything about luck.
I've never banked on it, and I'm afraid
of people who do. Luck to me is something else: hard work — and realizing
what is opportunity and what isn't.
Lucille Ball

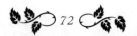

One of the things
I learned the hard way
was that it doesn't pay
to get discouraged.
Keeping busy and
making optimism a way
of life can restore your
faith in yourself.

Lucille Ball

I am not afraid of storms for I am learning how to sail my ship.

Louisa May Alcott

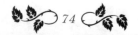

There is in every true woman's heart a
spark of heavenly fire which lies dormant
in the broad daylight of prosperity
but which kindles up and beams and
blazes in the dark hour of adversity.
Washington Irving

Birds sing after a storm; why shouldn't
people feel as free to delight in
whatever remains to them?
Rose Kennedy

It takes a lot of courage to show
your dreams to someone else.
Erma Bombeck

The best protection any woman
can have ... is courage.
Elizabeth Cady Stanton

Seeds of faith are always within us;
sometimes it takes a crisis to nourish
and encourage their growth.
Susan L. Taylor

Mother's Lesson #6:

Happiness

All mothers wish their children to be happy; thoughtful mothers show their children how.

Happiness, of course, is not so much a destination as it is a way of traveling. The following words of wisdom serve as guideposts for those travelers who make their journeys through life causes for celebration.

Cheerfulness, it would appear, is a matter which depends fully as much on the state of things within as on the state of things without and around us.

Charlotte Brontë

Happiness is a matter of one's
   most ordinary everyday mode of
consciousness — being busy and
lively and unconcerned with self.
                                    Iris Murdoch

If only we'd stop trying to be happy,
   we could have a pretty good time.
                                    Edith Wharton

One must never look for happiness:
   one meets it by the way.
                                    Isabelle Eberhardt

J oy is what happens to us when
we allow ourselves to recognize
how good things really are.
Marianne Williamson

A joy that's shared is
a joy made double.
John Ray

H appy is the man, and happy is he
alone, who can call today his own.
John Dryden

Happiness is good health
and a bad memory.
Ingrid Bergman

The greater part of happiness or misery
depends on our dispositions
and not our circumstances.
Martha Washington

Happy is he to whom, in the maturer season of life, there remains one tried and constant friend.

Anna Letitia Barbauld

Happiness to me is enjoying my friends and family.

Reba McEntire

There is only one happiness in life: to love and be loved.

George Sand

This is happiness: to be dissolved into
something complete and great.
Willa Cather

The three great essentials to happiness in
this life are something to do, something
to love, and something to hope for.
Joseph Addison

We must dare
to be happy....
Henri Frédéric Amiel

A bad temper and a fretful disposition
will make any state of life whatsoever
unhappy.

Cicero

There is only one way to happiness, and
that is to cease worrying about things
which are beyond the power of our will.

Epictetus

Too many wish to be happy
before becoming wise.

Suzanne Curchod Necker

Happiness doesn't depend upon who you are or what you have; it depends upon what you think.

Dale Carnegie

Gladly accept the gifts of the present hour.

Horace

Earth's crammed with heaven.

Elizabeth Barrett Browing

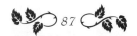

Be happy.
It's one way of
being wise.

Colette

Mother's Lesson #7:

Attitude

A mother's attitude is contagious. If she is optimistic and upbeat, the family will tend to be likewise. But if mother falls prey to pessimism and doubt, the family suffers right along with her.

Wise moms understand the power of positive thinking. These special women share a message of encouragement and hope with those around them, especially with their children. Then, by their mothers' words and actions, children learn this ironclad formula for living: attitude plus time equals reality.

Optimism is that
faith that leads to
achievement. Nothing
can be done without
hope and confidence.

Helen Keller

If you think you can, you can.
And if you think you can't,
you're right.

Mary Kay Ash

Despair is an evil counselor.

Sir Walter Scott

Worry is interest paid on trouble
before it falls due.

William Ralph Inge

No pessimist ever discovered the secrets
of the stars, or sailed to an uncharted
land, or opened a new heaven
to the human spirit.

Helen Keller

It is best to act with confidence,
no matter how little right
you have to it.

Lillian Hellman

There ain't nothing from the outside
can lick any of us.
Margaret Mitchell

All human wisdom is summed up
in two words: "wait" and "hope."
Alexandre Dumas

All times are beautiful for those who
maintain joy within them; but there is
no happy times for those
with disconsolate souls.
Rosalia Castro

The way in which we think of ourselves
has everything to do with how
our world sees us.

Arlene Raven

Happiness is not a matter of events;
it depends on the tides of the mind.

Alice Meynell

Human thoughts have a tendency
to turn themselves into their
physical equivalents.

Earl Nightingale

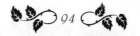

In the long run, we shape our lives and we shape ourselves. The process never ends until we die.

Eleanor Roosevelt

How very little can be done under the atmosphere of fear.

Florence Nightingale

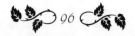

Act as if it were
impossible to fail.

Dorthea Brande

I am an optimist.
It does not seem too
much use to be
anything else.

Winston Churchill

You must do the thing you think
you cannot do.

Eleanor Roosevelt

A fool without fear is sometimes wiser
than an angel with fear.

Nancy Astor

They are able who think they are able.

Virgil

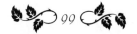

Live from miracle to miracle.

Artur Rubinstein

Live as if you like
yourself, and it
may happen.

Marge Piercy

It only seems as if you
are doing something
when you're worrying.

Lucy Maud Montgomery

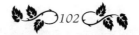

Mother's Lesson #8:

Life

Mothers not only give life, they teach it. On the following pages, we consider a collection of worldly wisdom that would make any mother proud.

Motherhood is the greatest privilege of life.

Mary Roper Coker

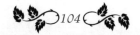

The role of mother is probably the most important career a woman can have.
Janet Mary Riley

The best academy is a mother's knee.
James Russell Lowell

A mother is not a person to lean on, but a person to make leaning unnecessary.
Dorothy Canfield Fisher

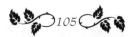

Live with no time out.

Simone de Beauvoir

Nothing is so often irretrievably missed
as a daily opportunity.

Marie von Ebner-Eschenbach

To be able to look back upon one's past
life with satisfaction is to live twice.

John Dalberg Acton

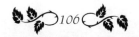

Life hurries past, too strong to stop,
too sweet to loose.

Willa Cather

The chief danger in life is that you may
take too many precautions.

Alfred Adler

Nobody's gonna live for you.

Dolly Parton

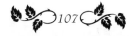

Plunge boldly into the thick of life!

Goethe

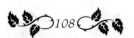

Be not afraid of life.
Believe that life is worth
living, and your belief
will help create the fact.

William James

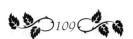

Assume responsibility
for the quality
of your own life.

Norman Cousins

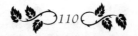

Life is what we make it.
Always has been.
Always will be.

Grandma Moses

Life is my college. May I graduate well
and earn some honors!
Louisa May Alcott

The worst sorrows in life are not in
its losses and misfortune but its fears.
A. C. Benson

When life kicks you, let it kick you
forward.
E. Stanley Jones

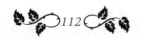

As long as one keeps searching,
the answers will come.
Joan Baez

Life is in the living, in the tissue
of every day and hour.
Stephen Leacock

Life isn't a matter of milestones,
but of moments.
Rose Kennedy

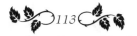

It is not enough to reach
for the brass ring. You must also enjoy
the merry-go-round.

Julie Andrews

There is no greater joy than that of
feeling oneself a creator. The triumph
of life is expressed by creation.

Henri Bergson

Life never becomes a habit to me.
It's always a marvel.

Katherine Mansfield

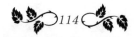

What we are is God's gift to us.
What we become is our gift to God.

Eleanor Powell

Life is the raw material.
We are the artisans.

Cathy Better

Do not take life
too seriously.
You'll never get out
of it alive.

Elbert Hubbard

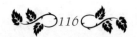

Sources

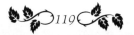

Sources

Sources

About the Author

Mary Carlisle Beasley is a writer who lives and works in Nashville, Tennessee and is the author of numerous books including several published by DELANEY STREET PRESS.

About
DELANEY STREET PRESS

DELANEY STREET PRESS publishes a series of books designed to inspire and entertain readers of all ages. DELANEY STREET books are distributed by Walnut Grove Press. For more information, call 1-800-256-8584.